LET'S THINK ABOUT

Sustainable Energy

Vic Parker

Raintree is an imprint of Capstone Global Library Limited, a company incorporated in England and Wales having its registered office at 7 Pilgrim Street, London, EC4V 6LB – Registered company number: 6695582

www.raintreepublishers.co.uk
myorders@raintreepublishers.co.uk

Text © Capstone Global Library Limited 2015
First published in hardback in 2014
The moral rights of the proprietor have been asserted.

Edited by John Paul Wilkins, Clare Lewis, and Brynn Baker
Designed by Tim Bond and Peggie Carley
Picture research by Liz Alexander and Tracy Cummins
Production by Victoria Fitzgerald
Originated by Capstone Global Library Ltd
Printed and bound in China by CTPS

ISBN 978 1 406 28264 1
18 17 16 15 14
10 9 8 7 6 5 4 3 2 1

British Library Cataloguing in Publication Data
A full catalogue record for this book is available from the British Library.

Acknowledgements
We would like to thank the following for permission to reproduce photographs: Alamy: © blickwinkel, 24, © David Grossman, 35, © Hideo Kurihara, 11, © Jeff Morgan07, 25, © Jim West, 20, © Kevin Allen, 29, © Visual Japan, 10; Corbis: © Hank Morgan - Rainbow/Science Faction, 18, © JACOB SLATON/Reuters, 7, © Jens Wolf/dpa, 32; Dreamstime: Jacek Chabraszewski, 41; Getty Images: JUNG YEON-JE/AFP, 30, 31, KAMBOU SIA/AFP, 26, 27, photovideostock, 42, Universal Images Group, 33; NASA: 43; Science Photo Library: HANS-ULRICH OSTERWALDER, 28, Styve Reineck, 9; Shutterstock: Antonio Abrignani, 4, B Brown, 6, Bart Everett, 37, Jesus Keller, 22, 23, miker, 38, 39, SasPartout, 19, scyther5, 8, TFoxFoto, 36; Superstock: Universal Images Group, front cover; Wikipedia: Gretar Ívarsson/Nesjavellir, 12, 13, Images of Africa Photobank, 16, U.S. Army Corps of Engineers, 14

Every effort has been made to contact copyright holders of material reproduced in this book. Any omissions will be rectified in subsequent printings if notice is given to the publisher.

All the Internet addresses (URLs) given in this book were valid at the time of going to press. However, due to the dynamic nature of the Internet, some addresses may have changed, or sites may have changed or ceased to exist since publication. While the author and publisher regret any inconvenience this may cause readers, no responsibility for any such changes can be accepted by either the author or the publisher.

Items should be returned on or before the last date shown below. Items not already requested by other borrowers may be renewed in person, in writing or by telephone. To renew, please quote the number on the barcode label. To renew online a PIN is required. This can be requested at your local library.
Renew online @ **www.dublincitypubliclibraries.ie**
Fines charged for overdue items will include postage incurred in recovery. Damage to or loss of items will be charged to the borrower. J 333·794

**Leabharlanna Poiblí Chathair Bhaile Átha Cliath
Dublin City Public Libraries**

Date Due	Date Due	Date Due

Contents

Some words are shown in bold, **like this.**
You can find out what they mean by looking in the glossary.

Sustainable energy

Scientists describe energy as "the ability to do work". Energy is everywhere, even though you cannot see it. Energy in sunlight makes plants grow. Energy in the wind moves clouds across the sky. Energy in food makes your body function.

Energy as fuel

Since ancient times humans have learned to use energy sources to help in our everyday lives. These energy sources are called fuels. For thousands of years we have burned wood as a fuel to give us light in the dark, warmth in the cold and heat to cook our food.

Burning wood releases heat and light energy. People use heat energy to cook and light energy to see in the dark.

Over the past 200 years, we have learned to use certain fuels to give us electricity and to power engines for machines. These fuels are oil, coal and natural gas. We call them fossil fuels because they were formed under the ground more than 100 million years ago from fossilized plants and animals.

Fueling the future

Humans have become so reliant on fossil fuels that we use billions of tonnes every year. Unfortunately, the processes involved in using the fuels release fumes into the air that are harming the planet. On top of this, one day the planet's reserves of fossil fuels will run out. They are a non-renewable source of energy.

In 1987 the United Nations said that we should aim for **sustainable energy**. This means countries should develop sources of energy that are renewable and that will not run out or harm the planet.

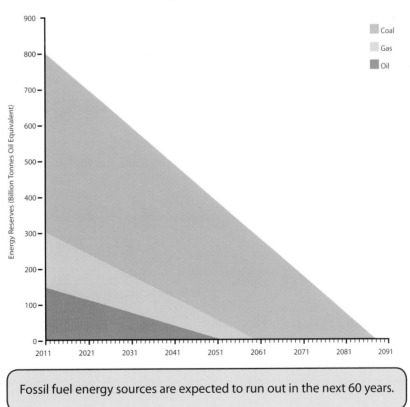

Fossil fuel energy sources are expected to run out in the next 60 years.

DID YOU KNOW?

In 2011 fossil fuels supplied 87 percent of the world's energy.

Future fuels

Let's look more closely at the problems linked with the use of fossil fuels. There are issues we should consider when thinking about alternative sources of fuel.

Environmental impact

Fossil fuel power plants burn oil, coal or natural gas. The heat produced is used to turn water into steam. The steam powers machines called turbines, and the turbines then power generators that produce electricity.

However, burning fossil fuels also releases harmful substances into the air, such as oxides. These oxides mix with water vapour and fall to Earth as acid rain. Acid rain is harmful to the environment.

Trees are cut down during the mining of fossil fuels. The environment suffers again when fossil fuels are then used.

Accidents at fossil fuel power plants also impact the environment. In 2013 an oil pipeline spilled in Arkansas and harmed wildlife.

The burning of fossil fuels releases a gas called carbon dioxide into the air. Carbon dioxide is one of several **greenhouse gases** that trap the Sun's heat around Earth. Scientific evidence shows that over the last century there has been an increase in carbon dioxide and that this is a major reason why Earth's surface temperature is rising. Scientists study the impacts of global warming, believing it to be causing ice in the polar regions to melt. The warming is also creating catastrophic weather. They say if carbon dioxide levels continue to rise, Earth's climate will reach devestating extremes.

WHAT DO YOU THINK?

According to the United States Environmental Protection Agency, natural gas produces only half as much carbon dioxide as coal. Should we develop our use of natural gas as well as developing renewable sources of energy?

Availability, cost, and the rising demand

The most commonly used fossil fuel is oil. More than 66 percent of the world's oil lies in Middle Eastern countries, such as Saudi Arabia and Iraq. Most other countries cannot produce enough of their own oil to meet demand, so they have to buy from the oil-rich countries. When Middle Eastern oil producers raise the price of oil, the rest of the world has no choice but to pay the higher price. This economic dependence is often the cause of arguments (and sometimes wars) between governments. The problem is expected to grow as more countries become industrialized and demand more energy.

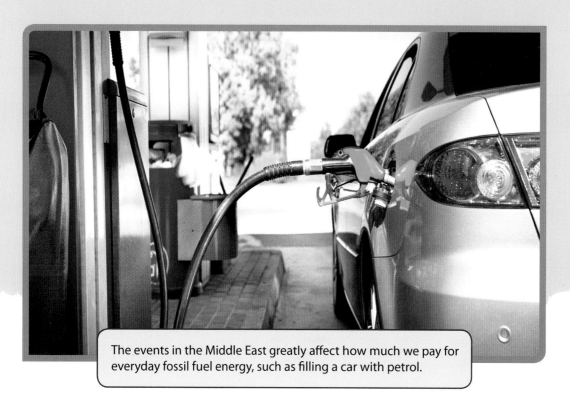

The events in the Middle East greatly affect how much we pay for everyday fossil fuel energy, such as filling a car with petrol.

An alternative to fossil fuels

The perfect alternative to fossil fuels should be renewable. It should not harm the environment when obtained or made, and it should not produce harmful waste. The renewable energy source should be widely available and able to meet the increasing demand at a reasonable price. Does such a fuel exist?

The challenge of meeting future energy demand

The International Energy Agency stated in 2012 that 1.3 billion people were without electricity, living mostly in four countries in developing Asia and six countries in Sub-Saharan Africa. However, as these countries become industrialized they will have a demand for electricity. But the IEA estimates that by 2030, almost 1 billion people will still be without electricity unless nearly £1 trillion is invested in energy supplies.

As villages like this one in Africa develop, the demand for electricity worldwide will increase.

Geothermal energy and hydropower

The first generation of renewable energy technologies was developed during the industrial revolution at the end of the 19th century. The resources used were widely and freely available, such as heat from the ground and river water. People have continued to improve technologies that use these energy sources.

Geothermal energy

At the centre of Earth, more than 5,633 kilometres (3,500 miles) down from the surface, is a ferociously hot core of molten iron. Scientists have estimated the temperature is as hot as the surface of the Sun! This heat warms a thick layer of molten rock called magma. Magma heats the rock and water in Earth's surface layer known as the crust. Some parts of the crust are thin or broken, creating bursts of heat that form hot springs, geysers and volcanoes.

These monkeys are bathing in the hot springs at Japan's Jigokudani Monkey Park.

Lardarello geothermal power plant in Tuscany, Italy, produces 10 percent of all the geothermal electricity in the world.

In other thin areas of crust, heat energy known as geothermal energy lies just below the Earth's surface. Wells are drilled down to areas of the hot rock where **reservoirs** of steam or very hot water are trapped.

DID YOU KNOW?

Iceland is rich in geothermal energy. In 2009, 66 percent of the country's power came from geothermal energy. Nine out of 10 households were heated geothermally.

The availability and cost of geothermal energy

Geothermal energy is considered renewable and reliable. The water involved in geothermal energy production can be reused and replenished by rain and melting snow. Heat from Earth's core is also available all year. Some countries have more geothermal resources than others, so geothermal power plants cannot be built everywhere. They also have high construction costs. However, after the initial investment, electricity costs to users are low and stable. The heat used to power a plant is free and comes from the ground beneath it. Geothermal energy plants are highly efficient.

The Nesjavellir geothermal power plant supplies heating and hot water for Reykjavík in Iceland.

Geothermal energy and the environment

Hazardous gases and materials can sometimes come to Earth's surface along with the hot water. However, they are properly disposed of so they do not become a pollutant. Geothermal energy does not burn fossil fuels, so no smoke is ever **emitted.** The production of carbon dioxide is therefore extremely low. Geothermal plants are also not as large as plants powered by fossil fuels, so building them has less of an impact on the environment.

Geothermal energy at home

People can buy geothermal heat pumps to install in their gardens to provide hot water and heat for their homes.

WHAT DO YOU THINK?

In early 2013 Hanne Krage Carlsen, a doctoral student at the University of Iceland, published research claiming that sulphur pollution from the Hellisheiði geothermal plant affected people with asthma. Do you think more research should be done into the health impact of geothermal energy?

Hydropower

Hydropower is energy from running or falling river water. It has been used since ancient times as a way to fuel machines, such as turning water wheels at mills. Today hydropower is largely used to create electricity, often described as hydroelectricity. The most common kind of hydroelectric plant uses a dam to collect river water in a reservoir. When the dam tunnels are opened, water rushes through them at great pressure – turning turbines, which then turn generators that produce electricity. As more tunnels in the dam are opened, larger amounts of water flows through, generating more electricity.

Canada is a country that has well-developed hydropower resources. There are two hydroelectric power plants at Niagara Falls, Ontario.

Availability of hydroelectric power

The cost of building a dam can be enormous. However, once built, the operation cost is low. The structures usually last 50 to100 years, and only a very small staff is needed to operate it. Also, the fuel it uses (river water) is free. For these reasons, hydroelectricity can have a low, steady cost. Hydropower is also considered a renewable source of energy because rivers can be replenished by rainfall and melting snow.

However some reservoirs, such as the Hoover Dam in Nevada, are not being replenished as much as in previous years. More tunnels are being opened to support the demand, but droughts have prevented rain from replenishing the river's water supply. If there are more droughts in the future due to climate change, this may affect the sustainability of hydropower.

DID YOU KNOW?

In 1878 English engineer William George Armstrong dammed rivers on his land, making his house the first in the world lit by hydroelectricity.

Hydropower is clean, but not green

Hydropower does not create pollution. However, the construction of a hydroelectric power plant can have a major impact on the environment. The building of a large dam floods a huge area upstream. Communities of people have to move and any wildlife that cannot do the same are destroyed. Habitats are flooded forever, with decaying trees producing greenhouse gases. A dam also affects life downstream. The regular flow of the river is altered, changing the quality and quantity of water. Plants and animals in those areas struggle to adapt. A dam can also prevent fish from moving up and downstream to their breeding grounds.

Lake Kariba was created by damming the Zambezi River in Africa, which borders the countries of Zambia and Zimbabwe. It is one of the world's largest artificial lakes and reservoirs, but its creators ensured it would be a haven for wildlife and tourism.

For hydropower to be sustainable, dams must be built with the environment in mind. Measures must be taken to protect river flows, water quality, fish passage and protection of threatened species.

WHAT DO YOU THINK?

The Three Gorges Dam is a massive hydroelectric power plant completed in 2012 on the Yangtze River in China. It supplies electricity to millions of people. However, the building of the dam has caused more than 1 million people to be moved from their homes and has flooded important cultural and archaeological sites. It is also causing significant changes to the environment, including endangering species such as the Chinese river dolphin. Do you think the dam should have been built?

Three Gorges Dam in China

Solar power and wind power

Solar power and wind power are considered second-generation renewable energy sources. These two sources were developed after the 1980s in an attempt to replace fossil fuels.

Solar power

For decades scientists and engineers have been researching ways of harnessing the immense energy in the Sun's rays. They have developed two efficient methods of supplying solar power to communities: photovoltaic and parabolic.

Photovoltaic solar thermal power is created by using hundreds of **photovoltaic cells** known as solar panels. The flat mirrored panels track the Sun and reflect the energy to a central grid or tower.

Parabolic solar thermal power is created by using long rows of U-shaped mirrors. The mirrors concentrate the Sun's heat energy on to a thin pipe of water running along the centres of the mirrors. The intense heat causes the water in the pipes to turn into steam. The steam is used to turn turbines, which then turn generators that produce electricity.

A parabolic solar thermal plant in Spain

WHAT DO YOU THINK?

In 2013 the country with the most solar panels on homes was Germany. One of the main reasons was because the German government made generous grants of money available to families to make the switch. Do you think your government should do the same? Or are there more important things for your government to spend its money on?

Fitting solar panels on a rooftop can heat hot water for the building, or supply electricity.

Ivanpah Valley in the Mojave Desert in California, is the largest solar power plant in the world.

Solar energy can be used all over the world

As long as the Sun beams down upon Earth, solar power will be available. It is a renewable source of energy. Solar power panels are ideal for powering individual homes or businesses in remote areas. However, they are available in any location as long as there is enough space for set up.

The downside is that solar power can be affected by cloudy weather, long periods of darkness in winter, or by pollution. Solar batteries were created to store extra electricity for when there is no sunshine. The main drawback to solar power is that the initial cost of the equipment is expensive.

Solar energy and the environment

Solar energy does not create any harmful **emissions** or produce any **toxic waste**. In small-scale uses, solar panels do not use any of the landscape, as they can be attached on to to pre-existing buildings. However, on a commercial scale, solar power plants take over vast areas of land in order to produce enough electricity for large numbers of people.

DID YOU KNOW?

A power company in Abu Dhabi, in the United Arab Emirates, built an enormous parabolic trough solar power station called Shams. It cost £239 million and aims to cut down on Abu Dhabi's high carbon dioxide emissions. The solar power plant's carbon dioxide reduction is the equivalent of planting 1.5 million trees every year!

Wind power

Wind is one of the oldest sources of power used by humans. Long ago, wind was used to fill sails to propel ships and to turn windmills to grind grain or pump water. Today's windmills are called wind turbines and can produce electricity. The clean and renewable energy in wind spins the rotor blades, which then spins the shaft and generator to produce electricity. A wind turbine can be small enough to be mounted on a pole outside your home, generating electricity for your household. Or it can be as tall as a 20-storey building and grouped together with other wind turbines on land or at sea to produce electricity on a large scale.

Groups of wind turbines that produce electricity on a large scale are known as wind farms.

Effects wind farms have on local people

Even though wind farms can stretch over a large area, each turbine does not take up much of the actual ground. Farmers can rent their farmland to wind power companies and still farm around the turbines. However, many people think wind turbines and their access roads spoil the beauty of the countryside. Locals often say they are bothered by the wind turbines producing a loud vibrating hum. Also, scientists are investigating whether the change in air pressure caused by wind turbines can cause illnesses. Some people living near them have complained of headaches, nausea, dizziness and other symptoms.

WHAT DO YOU THINK?

Some people think that wind turbines are ugly and spoil the beauty of nature. But some people think they are an elegant, clever idea. What is your opinion?

Effects wind farms have on wildlife

Early wind farms were constructed without detailed **environmental assessments**, so turbines often killed birds and bats that collided with the rotor blades. Wind farm planners now give wildlife proper consideration before building turbines. Researchers have found that modern wind farms kill only a fraction of the birds that die each year just flying into buildings. To protect bats, many wind farms stop operations in low wind conditions when bats are most active. Some turbines have radar transmitters, which keep bats a safe distance away.

A flock of geese fly in front of a wind turbine in the Netherlands.

Wind farm debates

Wind turbines are expensive, especially the ones constructed for the sea. Operating costs are low, however many people feel turbines are not worth the initial investment. The problem with wind power is that it comes and goes. Wind is very unreliable. It is possible to use batteries to store electricity for when the wind fails to blow. It is also possible to have a fossil-fueled generator as backup. However, both add significantly to the cost and to carbon dioxide emissions. There are many experts who are against wind farms, as well as many experts in support of them.

Wind power is a controversial form of renewable energy.

Biofuel and tidal power

The newest renewable energy technologies are described by the International Energy Agency as "third generation". They include energy from living things and from the sea.

Energy from living things

Energy that can be obtained from plants and animals is called biomass. The most common materials used are crops, wood, scrap paper, and animal droppings. Most biomass research today focuses on turning crops into fuel known as **biofuel**.

Biofuel: the issues

Biofuels can be made from crops such as wheat, corn, soy beans, and sugar cane. They are hailed by some experts as the ideal replacement for petrol, diesel and jet fuel. However, other experts have serious concerns.

Growing biofuel crops can provide income for poor families in rural farming areas of developing countries, such as India and China. However, allocating land for biofuel crops can mean a shortage of food crops. This raises food prices and results in hunger, as well as poor diet and health. Growing biofuel crops also requires large amounts of water, which many countries cannot provide. Finally, growing and processing crops requires energy from fossil fuels, resulting in carbon dioxide emissions. More research is needed to discover biofuels that are truly sustainable.

These workers in the Ivory Coast, West Africa, are growing crops for biofuel.

DID YOU KNOW?

Much of the petrol in the United States is blended with a biofuel called ethanol, which comes from corn. Biodiesel, made from palm oil, is widely available in Europe. Brazil has been making biofuel for decades. Some cars there can run on pure ethanol.

Power from the oceans

Energy from ocean tides can be used to produce electricity. The most common type of tidal plant operates by using a barrage, or dam. This closes off a tidal inlet and forms a reservoir. At high tide, gates in the barrage open and let seawater through. The captured water is then released back through a turbine, which turns a generator that produces electricity. In another type of tidal plant, turbines are submerged underwater. As tidal waters push through them, the rotor blades begin to spin.

Undersea tidal turbines work like wind turbines except they are spun by water, not wind.

Tidal power: the issues

Tidal power plants do not produce harmful emissions or waste, but environmental damage has been recorded. Changes in the quality of water have had an impact on sea life.

Tidal power plants cannot produce continuous energy, as they can only generate electricity during tidal flows. However tidal power is more reliable than other renewable energies because the tides are predictable. Even so, there are few locations that have the potential for commercially sized facilities, and the cost of establishing a tidal power plant is enormous.

Mud flats of the River Severn estuary near Bristol.

WHAT DO YOU THINK?

One of the biggest possible sites in the world for tidal power is on the River Severn estuary. If a tidal barrage was built here, it could generate five percent of the UK's electricity. However, the cost is estimated at over £15 billion! It would also prevent the tides going out as far, causing problems for the 65,000 birds that need the exposed mud flats to feed. If you lived there, would you support a Severn barrage?

Nuclear power

Everything in the universe is made up of tiny particles called atoms. Atoms are made up of even tinier particles known as neutrons, protons and electrons. An enormous amount of energy bonds together the neutrons, protons and electrons in each atom. If atoms of particular elements, such as uranium, are split, this enormous energy is released as heat. This is a reaction called **nuclear fission**. We can use nuclear fission as a source of fuel.

Nuclear power plants

Scientists have designed nuclear power plants in which the atoms in uranium can be split. They use a huge piece of equipment called a reactor. The resulting heat is used to boil water into steam, which powers turbines and generators, creating electricity.

Nuclear power plants are extremely expensive to build. However, once they are up and running, generating electricity in nuclear reactors is cheaper than using coal, oil or natural gas.

Nuclear power plants take up large areas of land. This one in Uljin, South Korea, is one of the largest in the world.

Nuclear power is risky

As part of the process by which they produce electricity, nuclear power plants also produce another type of energy called radiation. Radiation damages the cells of people, animals and plants. This can cause serious health problems and even death.

Nuclear power plants produce waste in many ways and much of it is **radioactive**. Radioactivity cannot be destroyed by burning it or washing it away. It has to decay naturally over thousands of years. Therefore, much nuclear power plant waste has to be packed into containers and stored under the ground or the ocean. Many people think this is very dangerous, due to the possibility of radiation leaking out.

Nuclear waste in underground storage will not become safe for at least 10,000 years.

Other risks

Nuclear power also includes the risk of accidents. A natural disaster could cause radiation to leak and spread. For instance, in March 2011 the Fukushima Daiichi nuclear power plant in Japan was damaged by an earthquake and then flooded by a tsunami. There were several reactor explosions before workers could close down the plant. The radiation that leaked out is likely to cause an increase in thyroid cancer in the local population in years to come. In July 2013 officials found a small amount of radioactive water from a storage tank that had been leaking into the Pacific Ocean ever since the accident.

The world's largest nuclear accident happened in 1986. A reactor exploded at the Chernobyl power plant in Ukraine. Vast areas of the former Soviet Union were devastated due to leaking radiation, which the wind carried across northern Europe.

Safety rules

Nuclear power plant owners and operators insist they have extremely tight construction and operating rules to ensure workers and local people are not at risk. Government agencies, however, are the ones responsible for ensuring that plant owners and operators comply with these strict health and safety regulations.

Controversies

Many people say that nuclear power is far from green. Besides the fact that nuclear power plants produce radioactive waste, the uranium they use to fuel the plant has to be mined, which damages the landscape and is non-renewable.

However, some experts do consider nuclear power to be green because the power plants produce little pollution and no carbon dioxide emissions.

Many countries are already invested in developing nuclear power. According to the World Nuclear Commission, in 2013, 43 more countries were considering establishing nuclear power in the near future.

Safe and secure

In 2013 the United States National Energy Institute stated, "The nuclear energy industry is one of the nation's safest industries – protected by multiple backup safety systems, robust physical defences, and plant security forces with rigorous training."

Many people feel so strongly against nuclear power that they campaign to abolish the industry.

WHAT DO YOU THINK?

Would you be happy to live near a nuclear power plant? Do you think the advantages of nuclear power outweigh the disadvantages?

Energy efficiency

The goal of sustainable energy is not just about finding renewable, available, green and clean energy sources. It also involves reducing the overall amount of energy we need to run products and services. This is called being energy efficient. Energy efficiency is vital if the world is going to be able to meet its rapidly growing demand for energy.

Saving energy

Governments can encourage everyone to employ energy-saving technologies by offering savings and special deals to those who do. For instance, governments can reward construction companies for using energy efficient designs and materials in new buildings. They can offer grants to individuals to insulate their homes to prevent heat loss and to establish renewable energy technologies, such as using wind turbines. Governments can also invest in improving old buildings and updating public transport systems.

Updating windows and insulation in your own home will reduce energy consumption.

Responsibility

However, it's not just governments' responsibility. We all have a responsibility to do what we can to save energy, regardless of where it comes from. If we all do what we can to be energy efficient, our efforts will add up to the huge energy savings our planet needs!

Driving big trucks or vehicles that run on petrol and diesel fuel produces a lot of carbon dioxide. Many people have made the switch to more energy-efficient cars.

Efficiency ratings

How can you tell which household appliances, such as refrigerators, are the most energy efficient? Most countries have a labelling system, providing a graded level for each appliance. The labels also give a close estimate to how much energy the appliance will need to operate for a full year.

The impact of energy efficiency

According to the International Energy Agency, "The world is not on course for a sustainable future ... but this alarming outlook can be changed." If energy efficiency is improved in homes, businesses, and transportation, in addition to researching renewable energies and biofuels, the world's energy needs in 2050 could be reduced by one-third. These changes would reduce carbon dioxide levels in the atmosphere by 16 percent, helping to win the race against global warming and climate change.

This energy-efficient bus produces zero greenhouse gas emissions. Energy efficiency can play a major part in helping the environment.

Energy efficiency can also help countries. By becoming energy efficient, they can reduce the amount of energy they need to import, reducing their dependence on other nations. They would be able to develop and industrialize without spending as much money on energy.

Individuals also benefit by reducing their personal energy consumption. The more energy people use, the higher their utility bills will be because the demand for production will then be higher. If people use less energy, production costs would be lower, utility bills would be lower, and it would help to save the environment.

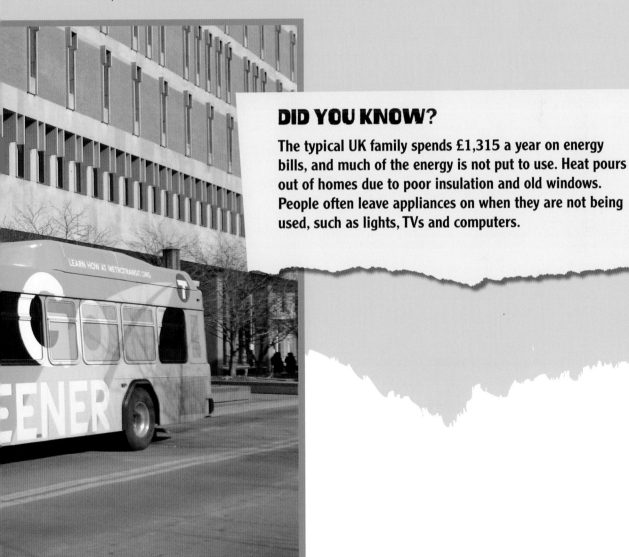

DID YOU KNOW?

The typical UK family spends £1,315 a year on energy bills, and much of the energy is not put to use. Heat pours out of homes due to poor insulation and old windows. People often leave appliances on when they are not being used, such as lights, TVs and computers.

Reducing your energy consumption

Here are some ways that you can be more energy efficient. Encourage your family and friends to do the same.

- Turn off the lights when you leave a room.

- Turn off electrical appliances when you are no longer using them, such as TVs and computers.

- Do your homework near a large window, rather than having a light on.

- If the weather is chilly and you are cold, try adding an extra layer of clothes or wrap up in a blanket before turning up the heat.

- If you only need to travel a short distance, walk or ride your bike instead of taking a car.

- Once a week, enjoy a salad or sandwich instead of using energy to cook a hot meal.

- Donate old personal items instead of throwing them away. If someone else buys your used books, toys and clothes that means they did not have to buy it new. Recycling goods saves energy used for manufacturing, transportation, and in retail stores.

- For the same reason, consider buying second-hand items instead of new ones.

WHAT DO YOU THINK?

Which energy efficiency measures do you think you can achieve?
Which do you think you can encourage others to achieve?
Are there any you think are unrealistic? Why?

You can reduce your energy use by finding ways to have fun that do not use electricity at all.

Is sustainable energy possible?

At the moment there is no single sustainable energy source that can answer all of our needs. Each one has its advantages, disadvantages and compromises. Fossil fuels are non-renewable and emit carbon dioxide. Geothermal energy is not available everywhere and creates some toxic by-products. Hydropower destroys land and damages river habitats, and it is not reliable. Solar power can also be unreliable, is expensive to establish and large-scale operations take over large areas of land. Wind power is unreliable, expensive to implement and backup fossil fuel energy systems emit carbon dioxide. Biofuels can contribute to food shortages, water shortages and carbon emissions. Tidal power is only possible at a few sites and power plants are expensive to establish. Nuclear power plants are even more expensive to build and they produce radioactive waste.

Living green and reducing energy consumption is how we can help the survival of our planet.

Looking to the future

Some say **nuclear fusion** might provide the answer to a truly sustainable energy source. Nuclear fusion is a process where multiple atoms join together and release energy. The fuel used is deuterium, which is readily and cheaply available throughout the world and virtually inexhaustible. Deuterium is taken from water. Just a thimbleful of deuterium is equal to approximately 20 tonnes of coal in energy production. Fusion would not emit carbon dioxide or atmospheric pollution. Also, fusion could produce much less radioactive waste than fission, and would be radioactive for tens of years rather than tens of thousands of years. However, more research still needs to be done.

The future of our planet depends on how we manage our energy needs.

Debate it!

Are you ready to debate some of these issues with your friends?
If so, these five tips may help.

1. Be prepared. Do some research before you begin, and make a list of points you plan to debate. Then think of arguments on the other side. Then you'll be prepared when your friend mentions them.

2. State your opinions clearly. It's useful to provide examples and statistics.

3. Listen carefully. After all, you cannot respond effectively unless you understand exactly what your friend is saying. You can ask your friend to repeat the comment or provide further information.

4. Keep your cool. In a good debate, there is no clear winner or loser. You will win some points and lose others. You may even find that some of your friend's comments make sense. That's not bad. It shows that you are keeping an open mind.

5. Have fun! Debate is a great way to explore the issues.

Glossary

biofuel fuel made from crops such as corn or soy beans

emissions harmful gases or fumes released from something

emit to release

environmental assessment determining the possible impacts that a proposed project may have on the environment

greenhouse gas air pollutant in Earth's atmosphere that traps radiation and is responsible for the greenhouse effect and global warming

nuclear fission when an atom is split, releasing an enormous amount of energy

nuclear fusion when atoms are combined, releasing an enormous amount of energy

photovoltaic cell solar panel that uses sunlight to produce an electric current or voltage caused by electromagnetic radiation

radioactive emissions of dangerous radiation as a consequence of a nuclear reaction

reservoir place where water is collected and stored

sustainable energy capable of being maintained, supported, and replenished without exhausting natural resources or causing ecological damage

toxic waste poisonous materials, especially chemical

Find out more

Books

Harnessing the Sun's Energy (Why Science Matters), Andrew Solway
(Heinemann Library, 2008)

How Can We Save Our World? (Sustainable Energy), Angela Royston
(Franklin Watts, 2009)

Sustaining Our Natural Resources, Jen Green
(Raintree, 2011)

Websites

**http://www.bbc.co.uk/schools/gcsebitesize/geography/energy_resources/
energy_rev1.shtml**
Read more about the arguments for and against renewable energy resources on
this BBC website.

http://www.ourplanet.org.uk
Visit this website for more in-depth information about renewable energy sources
and climate change.

Further research

To find out more about sustainable energy, you and a grown-up can search the internet by using keywords such as these:

- biofuels
- energy efficiency
- future fuels
- geothermal power
- hydropower
- nuclear power
- renewable energy
- solar power
- sustainable energy
- tidal power
- wind power

Or you can find your own keywords by choosing words from the book.

Where to search

Type your keywords into a search engine. A search engine looks through millions of websites that have information matching the keywords. You will find the best matches on the top of the first page.

Search tips

There are billions of websites on the internet, so it can be difficult to find exactly what you are looking for. These tips will help you find useful websites more quickly:

- Know what you want to find
- Use simple keywords
- Only use names of people, places, or things.
- Put quotation marks around words that go together, such as "sustainable energy"

Index